The
Boy Who Fell
Off the
Mayflower

or
John Howland's
Good Fortune

P.J. LYNCH

CANDLEWICK PRESS

LONDON

London was a fine city when I was there. Greatest city in the whole world. Smelled bad, I must say, but it was huge and busy and exciting for a young lad like me.

It was all because of the king that we had to leave England. Him and his bishops didn't like the way our people chose to worship. None of their business, I said. They jailed our leaders and harassed us till we had to leave our homeland to live in Holland. But the youngest among us now seemed more Dutch than English, and, with the fear of a new war with the Spanish coming, our elders decided we'd take our chances in the New World.

We came to London to rent ourselves a ship with a Captain Jones and his crew. We were loading her up with provisions for the long voyage to America. I had hoped for a day and a half to go and see my mother and brothers in Fenstanton, but my master said we were too pressed for time.

When I wasn't running all around London ordering barrels of this and bales of that, my master, John Carver, had me copying out lists of supplies and letters to the businessmen who were lending us money to fund our voyage. Many's the year we'd be working to pay them off.

When our ship was nearly loaded, Master Carver sent me to find the Warwick Inn, up by the city wall beyond the cathedral. I was looking for a certain gentleman.

In the noisy throng of Londoners, a tall white-bearded man stood out. "Elder William Brewster?" I whispered to him. "Master Carver sent me for you. We leave London with the dawn tide."

"I remember you well from Holland, John," he replied. "Take me to the ship, lad, and let's be quick. There is danger for us here."

Sure enough, there were shifty-looking characters all about, and dozens of the king's militiamen were in the streets. If they had known that I was with one of the leaders of the Separatists, the very man who published all those pamphlets against the king and his bishops, we would have been done for. They would have chopped off Elder Brewster's head and mine and stuck them up on spikes on London Bridge for sure.

We stuck to the back lanes and alleyways, and by the time we made it down to the wharf, it was already dark. The taverns nearby were noisy with sailors and longshoremen, but the quays were quiet. At last we came to our ship.

She was being loaded by lamplight now. Casks of beer, sacks of onions and cabbages, boxes of salted herring, and barrels of corned beef. Tasty stuff. Some of the passengers were still getting their chests and their bits of furniture on board. The sheep and goats and chickens were waiting till last.

My master shook William Brewster's hand fit to shake it off, then hurriedly guided us across the gangway. "Thank the Lord you are safe, William," he said. "Welcome aboard the *Mayflower*."

THE MAYFLOWER

Outside Master Carver's cabin, I unrolled my mattress and tried to get some sleep. I don't think I'd slept even an hour before I heard the great clanking of the windlass as they hoisted the anchor.

I ran up on deck for a last look at London. Only a few lights were lit, and the big ship made hardly a sound drifting down on the tide away from the sleeping city.

One of our sailors bellowed a farewell across the river to a woman on the wharf. A coarse shout came back: *"Godspeed!"*

And I thought of my mother's gentle voice: *"Godspeed, John."*

The sun was up by the time we reached Gravesend, where the river widened. The crew was busy unfurling the sails to catch the morning breeze. I was enjoying the fresh air when a burly sailor came over to me.

"You're the boy that runs the messages, ain't you?"

"Yes, sir, I am. . . . John Howland's my name. . . ."

"Never mind that! Just get below and tell your boss that Bob Coppin — that's me, the first mate — orders that the passengers are to keep down 'tween decks now we're under way. We'll let you know when you can come up for air. And keep it quiet with all that praying!" With that, he stomped off, laughing.

"I'll be pleased to take your message, Master Coppin," I called after him. "You will find, sir, that we are civil people, and we hope to give no offense to God or man. We hope only for a measure of civility in return!"

The first mate stopped laughing. He turned around and looked long and hard at me. Then he gave me a nod and said, "Right you are . . . Master Howland."

THE *SPEEDWELL*

We made good time skirting round the coast to Southampton, and there we waited till our smaller ship, the *Speedwell,* arrived from Holland with the rest of our company. The two vessels were drawn up side by side and lashed together, and there was a joyful welcome as we met our old friends again.

William Bradford, Captain Standish, and the other important folks gathered around my master. I went to chat with the other servants. The lads were excited about the adventure ahead of us.

"I heard that the trees there are five times bigger than in England," said Bill Butten, the doctor's servant, "and the rivers are full to the brim with fat fish just begging to be caught."

"There's a parcel of land and a fine suit of clothes awaiting me next spring," said Roger Wilder. He had only six months left of his indenture. "I'll have my pick of all the free English girls in Virginia to wed. Poor old Howland here will have to wait another three years."

"You may laugh, Roger, but when my time is through, I'll be jumping on the first ship headed back for England. London is where I'll make my fortune. Perhaps I'll open a shop selling soap and candles to foolish folk who want to go live in the New World!"

"Now there's a fine young lady. Might make a good wife for me in a year or three," said Bill, and he nodded toward a skinny girl who was playing nearby with the little'uns.

"Master Tilley will have your hide if you go near his little Lizzy," said Roger. "When she comes of age, he'll be wanting her to marry the doctor, not the doctor's skivvy."

We all laughed and the girl glanced over. Then the children dragged her off to see the baby goats and piglets being brought on board.

It took weeks before our two ships set out from Southampton, but we had hardly gone ten leagues when our troubles began.

Speedwell! Never was a ship less well named. Every time that little ship was put under a swell of canvas, she became as open and leaky as a sieve. We had to limp along the south coast of England, stopping to patch her up several times. Finally we put in to Plymouth harbor, and it was decided that we must leave *Speedwell* there and proceed with only the *Mayflower.*

Bill told me his master wasn't keen to go on. He said that our supplies were near half eaten up before we had even left England.

"Half gone already, John! We're sailing into winter. What will we eat when we get to Virginia?"

"Don't forget those fat fish just begging to be caught," I joked. But a good many of our company decided to stay behind.

"We've sold all our possessions in Holland," said Master Carver. "There is no going back for us, John! Trust in the Lord with all your heart, for He favors our endeavor."

So we committed ourselves to the will of God and put to sea at last under a prosperous wind with all of us on the one good ship. Bob Coppin barked his orders, and the sailor boys were busy, shinning up the rigging and unfurling the sails. The wind snapped the canvas taut, and the old ship's timbers creaked as she cut smartly through the waves.

Many's the tear that was shed as we waved farewell to our friends, to Plymouth, and to England.

THE VAST AND FURIOUS OCEAN

Half our company now were Strangers. That's what we called them. They were Christians indeed, just not the same kind as us. A lot of the Strangers were good folk. Like us, they had little to keep them in England and high hopes for what future they might make for themselves in the New World.

No one stayed strangers long, the way we were crowded together between decks. Some of the better-off passengers had a cabin to themselves, but most of the families just had a blanket or two hung up on a rope to give them a bit of privacy.

For some few days, the weather stayed fair, and Bob Coppin called for me to relay a message that we were allowed on deck to stretch our legs. Bob was a decent sort, but most of the sailors cursed at us and mocked those of us afflicted with seasickness.

Our time at sea was tedious and uncomfortable. As servants, we at least had a few jobs to keep us busy. I would often be asked by Master Carver to fetch a box of candles from the hold or take a message up to the captain or copy out some accounts.

As we sailed on, we encountered fierce storms, and we didn't get up to see the sky for days on end. Each big wave that broke over the ship drained down through the decks on top of us. We were wet and cold all the time, and we couldn't even look forward to a hot meal. All we had to eat was hard tack and the odd bit of salt pork.

In spite of it all, Lizzy Tilley remained cheerful. She and the other girls played games with the little'uns to keep their spirits up. Elder Brewster led us in prayer and the singing of hymns. Most of the Strangers joined in.

Some weeks out from Plymouth, we were caught in a really cruel storm. Everyone held tight to a rope or a bulkhead, and the little'uns were firmly strapped in. Of a sudden, the ship reeled right over, and Lizzy Tilley rolled out of a bunk and landed at my feet.

"Are you all right, miss?" I said, helping her up.

"Yes, thank you, Master Howland."

As she spoke, the ship keeled over the other way. There was a loud wrenching sound, and a torrent of water poured in on us.

"Hold tight!" I thrust a rope into her hands and hurried off with the men to check the damage. So Lizzy Tilley knew my name.

One of the main beams holding up the deck had buckled, and now the planks were flapping loose in the wind. Roger said he heard the captain talking about turning back for England. I'd have been in favor of that myself, but I held my peace.

William Bradford spoke. "We will not put about! In the hold we have an iron screw for raising roof timbers. We can use it to jack the beam into position." He looked at us then, and his eyes lit on me. "Get a lantern, John. We're going below."

We made our way down into the cold and darkness of the hold to look for the jack among all the casks and chests and furniture. When we found it, we slung a stout rope around it. The men above took most of the weight, and Bradford and I heaved from below. It was a mighty job to lift that jack up through the hatches with the ship rolling nearly onto her beam ends.

Once the screw was fixed in place, we turned it and hoisted the timber back into position. The carpenter quickly hammered a strong post under it. After a good caulking of the planks, the ship was sound enough to proceed.

MAN OVERBOARD

In quiet times, Bob Coppin would stop to tell me his tall tales and share an orange or a cut of pork jerky with me.

"When your time with Master Carver is up, maybe you'll become a seaman yourself. There's always a place for a keen lad in my crew. You might have a few adventures of your own, eh, John?"

"Thank you but no, sir," I replied. "I'm not one for adventures. It is my intention to return to London at the first opportunity and perhaps to go into business there."

"Business, is it?" Bob Coppin smiled. "I believe you might do it too . . . with a bit of good fortune."

Mostly though, the mate and his crew were hard at work fighting the weather. Sometimes it was so bad, they had to let the ship lie under bare poles, point her into the wind, and hope she would weather the storm.

It was just such a time when I took it upon myself to go up on deck, despite the order that we all stay below. I was seeking a bit of relief from the foul stench 'tween decks. I was hardly up through the hatch when a huge wave hit and sent me flying over the side.

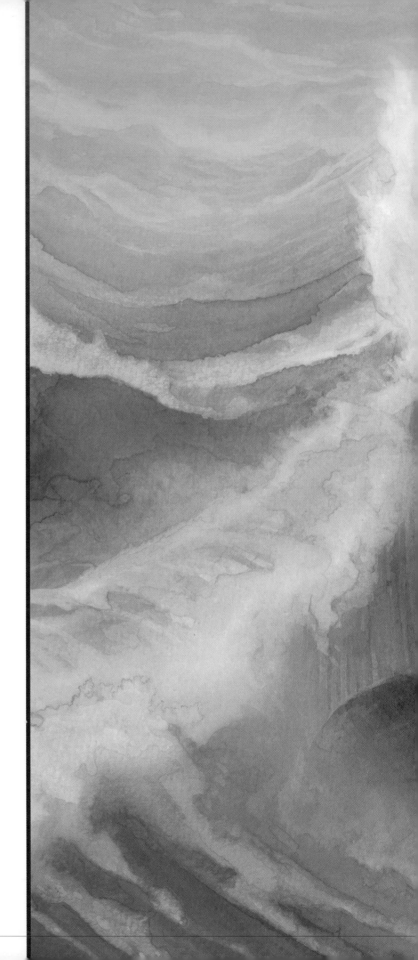

Down and down I went into the darkness under the icy waves. It was quiet down there, no raging wind or rain like up above. A strong current was dragging me deeper and farther away from the ship.

The deeper it got, the darker it got, and soon I wasn't feeling the cold. I just wanted to shut my eyes and go to sleep for a hundred years.

"Wake up, John," said my mother's voice. *"Wake up, dreamer!"*

Far up above, I saw the *Mayflower*'s keel. I thought, *That's my ship. . . . She's taking me to America!* A flash of lightning lit up a long rope trailing down from the ship. I pulled myself over toward it. My lungs were bursting now, but I caught hold of the rope and held on tight in the freezing water. Luckily for me, one of the crew had seen me fall overboard. Bob and his sailor boys hauled me in like a big fish. Then they were shouting and scolding me and rolling me over a barrel to get the seawater out of my lungs.

I've no recollection at all of what happened after that or over the next few days, but Roger told me that my master had me brought to his cabin and that Mistress Carver herself nursed me till I was well.

Elder Brewster announced to everyone that it was the Lord God himself who put that rope in my hand. "'And the Lord brought them forth with a mighty hand and an outstretched arm, and with miraculous signs and wonders.'"

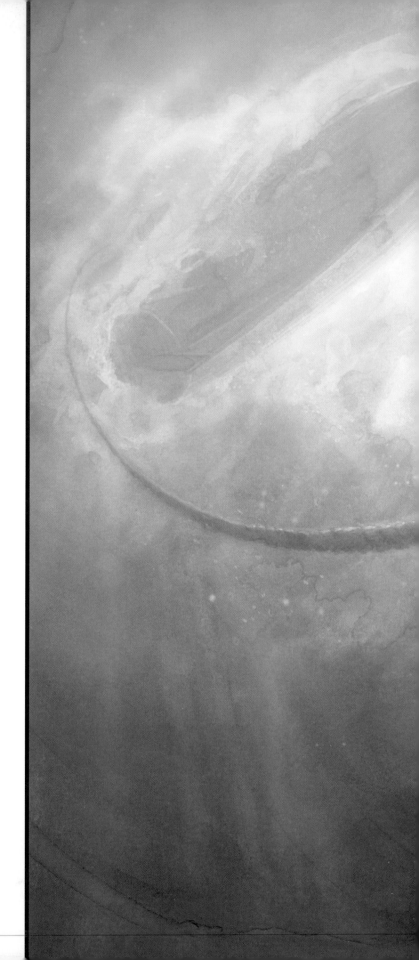

It was a week before I was on my feet again, and the first day I went back among the passengers, I noticed a great alteration in them. Two months lying wet and weary in that unwholesome old ship were taking their toll.

Folks were glad to see that I was all right, and they clapped me on the back, but some of them couldn't rise in their bunks, the pains in their joints were that bad.

When old Master Chilton joked about me trying to swim home to England, his laugh turned into a wheezy cough, and I saw that his gums were all rancid and black. Then Bill Butten took a bad fever, and on the third day, he died. Not a thing his master the doctor could do about it.

As Bill's shrouded body was pitched into the sea, I saw Lizzy Tilley and some of the younger ones crying. I wondered if she might have cried if it was me that was dead.

Elder Brewster spoke to them sharply.

"Enough of the tears, children! The Lord God will be our guide even unto death. He has called William Butten to his heavenly rest. We must not question His plan."

LAND HO!

One morning in early November, the shout went up: "Land ho!" Those that were able rushed up on deck to see what America looked like. It didn't look like much to have crossed a vast ocean and a sea of troubles for . . . a gray stretch of sandy cliffs with a few scrubby trees. But all of us passengers were right joyous, thinking that soon our feet would be on dry land again.

Bob Coppin was shaking his head and grumbling. "That ain't Virginia, lad," he said to me. "I was up and down this coast with Captain Smith. Those storms have driven us two hundred miles north of where you folks want to be. That there's Cape Cod."

Well, there was great debating between our leaders and the captain about whether we should land here or head south. It was decided that we should head to Virginia. So we tacked around and sailed south.

At first the tide and the wind pushed us along briskly, but before long we fell among treacherous currents and roaring breakers. It got so bad that many of us feared that now, within sight of the New World, all would be lost. But by God's will we were delivered from those perils, and the captain guided the ship back to Cape Cod's safe harbor, swearing that he would not risk those waters again.

Our elders and the most important of the Strangers met then in the captain's cabin. Outside, all the servants and the women were straining to hear what was going on within. I had my ear to the door.

"What are they saying now, John?" whispered Mistress Carver.

"Seems that some of the Strangers reckon we won't be bound by any charter at all if we settle here and not in Virginia," I said. "Say they might go their own way once we're ashore."

"They wouldn't!" she answered. "None of us will survive if we don't stay together."

The arguing inside went on for a good while longer, then suddenly Master Carver opened the door and I nearly fell into the cabin. He was surprised for a moment, then he clasped his wife's hands and said, "May God sustain me, Kate, it is decided that I am to be the colony's governor." Mistress Carver looked not a bit pleased at this news.

"Our first duty, John," said Master Carver, turning to me. "Get your ink and quill. We have a new charter for you to copy out in your best hand."

I carefully wrote out the words of a solemn compact that said we would govern ourselves by agreement among ourselves for the good of us all. Fine words, and all the men that were able signed it, even me and the other servants.

AMERICA

Now, young Master Howland," William Bradford said, throwing me a sword and scabbard, "arm yourself well. We're going ashore."

As soon as we set foot on dry land, we fell on our knees and blessed the God of Heaven, who had brought us over that vast and furious ocean and delivered us from all our perils.

I confess that while the others were praying, I was keeping a sharp eye out for any more perils that might have been lurking in the scrub. We began to explore, and we found the place to be a naked, barren wilderness.

Our search of the area revealed no suitable place for habitation. Nor did we know how to find or meet the native people we knew inhabited this land. Once we saw a party of them running across a beach, but they were a long way off, and though we called to them and pursued them for some miles, we could not find any of them.

We did find some houses seemingly abandoned, though, and under a mound of sand, we dug up a great basket filled with seed corn. Captain Standish said to load it up into a big kettle that was there, and we carried it back to the ship. My conscience was troubled about that.

After the long tedium of the voyage, we were all busy now about the ship and on shore. Our people ferried back and forth to refresh themselves on dry land and returned to the ship with firewood and fresh water. The women took the chance to wash clothes and bedding and laid it out clean on the rocks to dry in the winter sun. Even the young ones made themselves useful helping to carry the animals to shore for some fresh spring water.

Our biggest job was fixing up our large sailing boat, the shallop, which had been cut in four pieces for stowing between decks. While hoisting a beam alongside Elder Brewster, I said, "I know they are heathens, sir, but the corn that we took . . . Well, that seemed a lot like stealing to me."

"John," he replied, "the Lord has seen our need and has answered our prayers. Don't you recognize God's Providence, which He has placed before your eyes? We will repay the Indians fourfold, if we can ever find them."

Truth is we were getting desperate, not only for food but for a place to settle. Each day that passed, more of our people on board the *Mayflower* fell sick.

Bob Coppin recalled a likely place from his time mapping with Captain Smith and a party of us set out in the shallop to find it, but we made slow progress. The cold wind lashed the hail in our faces, and the water froze on our clothes and made them like coats of iron. When it got dark, we put ashore to rest the night. We built a rough stockade for shelter. We got little sleep, though, for the hideous cries we heard in the dark.

In the morning, one of our company ran screaming, *"Indians! Indians!"* and straightaway a hail of arrows came zipping all around us. We rushed to our muskets and fired back.

Bob and some of our men got separated down at the boat. They had muskets but no firebrand to fire them with. I ran to the fire, grabbed a burning log, and scrambled down the beach to our fellows, who took fire and started shooting at our attackers.

We could see the Indians' leader fearlessly letting fly his arrows from behind a tree only half a musket shot away from us. "That must be the man whose corn you took!" shouted Bob. Captain Standish finally hit the very tree itself, and the Indian took flight with a great cry, the rest of his band behind him.

So it pleased God to give us deliverance from our attackers without killing a one of them or getting a scratch on one of our own.

SAFE HARBOR

We collected ourselves and loaded into the shallop right quick and cast off, heading north along the coast. We sailed with the icy winds whipping around us all that day without seeing a harbor, a river, or even a creek.

A squall blew up of a sudden, and with Bob Coppin and me leaning on the tiller to steer us away from the rocks, the hinges of our rudder broke. There was nothing we could do but try to steer with our oars. Over the din of the storm, Bob shouted, "Be of good cheer, lads. I see it . . . I see the harbor!" and we cut in for the break in the shoreline.

The wind behind us now was so strong that our mast shattered, and with our rudder hanging loose, the shallop was tossed like a toy from one huge breaker to the next. It was only by God's mercy that our boat was borne into the shelter of a small island rather than being broken into pieces on the rocky shore.

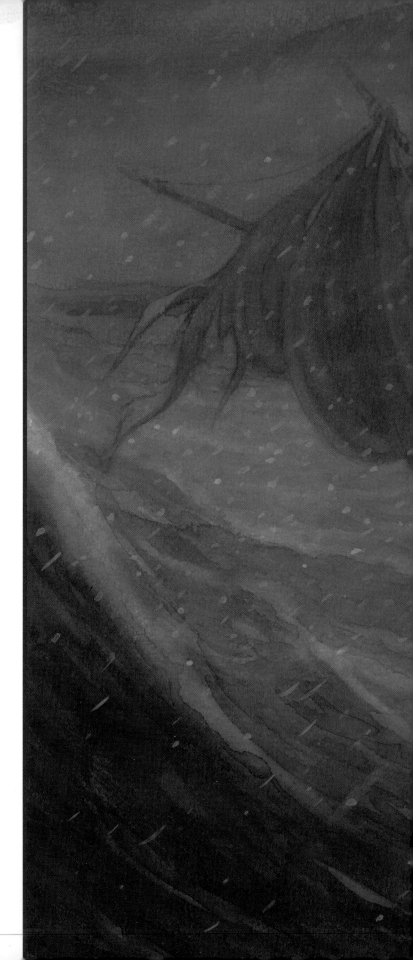

Turned out it wasn't the place Bob had thought, but when we had a chance to sound the harbor and survey the land around, we agreed that this was indeed a most hopeful place for our settlement.

It seemed to us the Lord had saved us from the deluge and carried us here, for we found that the land had already been cleared for cornfields. There were graves and bones aplenty, yet there were no living Indians to be seen.

We repaired the shallop as best we could and sailed back to the *Mayflower* to tell of our discovery. But there was grim news at the ship. In the six days we had been exploring, more of our people had taken sick, and more still had perished. Old Master Chilton and William Bradford's wife, Dorothy, were among them.

CHRISTMAS DAY, 1620

Master Jones sailed the *Mayflower* up to our new situation. He announced to us that the place was called New Plymouth on Captain Smith's map. Now we knew that God's hand had guided us across the ocean from Plymouth, our last port in England, to Plymouth, our new home in New England.

I was part of a landing party of twenty put ashore to build houses, but we were tormented by foul weather and made little progress. I never thought things could get more miserable than on the ship, but as we looked through the rain and sleet to where the *Mayflower* was anchored in the bay, we envied the relative comfort of our friends still on board.

Sometimes we saw Indians watching us from the dark of the forest. At night we'd hear terrible cries that would make us shudder to our very bones.

One morning when Captain Standish woke us, he was less gruff than usual. "It's Christmas Day, lads. God save you all. Looks to be a dry one. We'll get those gables built if it stays good."

It warmed us up to heft an ax and pull a saw, and before long we had hoisted up the frame of the first house. At noon we stopped for thin soup and ship's biscuits. Standish gave us each an extra piece of salted cod, too. "Don't tell Elder Brewster!"

As we chewed, I remembered the last Christmas I spent with my mother and my brothers. Games and songs with Arthur and little Henry. Mutton pies and roasted goose. A hug and a smile and a "Merry Christmas, John," from my mother. Roger pulled me to my feet. "Come on, dreamer. Back to work."

In two weeks, the house was built. Before the thatching was pinned down, Roger and I had bagged a spot for our mattresses in the loft. It was smokier up there and it made Roger's cough worse, but at least it was dry. Downstairs, the rain sloshed in and the floor was wet mud.

Before long, though, we had to make room for the sick. Captain Jones wanted them off the ship. So Roger and I were back under canvas.

At first the women tended to the afflicted while the men worked on the houses, but soon most of the women were ill, too. At times only six or seven of us remained well enough to tend to the others.

Lizzy and the women were up before dawn boiling dried peas for pottage, but those that were poorly ate little or nothing. Most of our time was spent cleaning the sick and washing their filthy bedding. I helped with Lizzy's father and her uncle, and then with Roger. The work was so loathsome that I thought it a blessing to be ordered out into the cold and rain to fell trees and split planks.

A few of the sick, like William Bradford, recovered, but in spite of all the care that young Lizzy Tilley gave to her family, they all died. One after the other. Mother, father, aunt, and uncle.

We buried our dead at night so the Indians might not see our true weakness. Our great adventure was becoming a nightmare of sickness, death, and danger.

By the time winter was over, Roger had died, and so had most of the other servant lads, too. Of one hundred and odd persons, scarce fifty of us were left.

WELCOME, ENGLISHMEN!

With the arrival of spring, the bitterness had gone from the north wind. We had fewer sick folk and more houses built.

One morning, a tall fine-looking Indian walked boldly into our village. He walked right up to Captain Standish and said, "Welcome, Englishmen!"

His name was Samoset. He had learned some English from the men on the fishing boats who visited this coast. As he was right friendly and peaceable, we gave him food and some little gifts. Later he came back with other Indians.

One was Squanto, who spoke English near as well as me. He told us about his own people, the Patuxet, who had lived in the place where we'd settled. He told us about the mighty sachem who ruled that land, the great King Massasoit of the Wampanoag, and of his many warriors.

MASSASOIT

It was arranged that Massasoit himself should come to our settlement, and we welcomed him as royally as if he was the cousin of the king of England. Mistress Carver and the other women prepared our finest foods, and it was my job to serve it to the governor and the Indian sachem.

It was months since I had seen such a spread. Massasoit must have seen how hungrily I looked at it, for he smiled and offered me a leg of the roast duck. I confess I took it and ate as much as I could before my mistress scolded me and took it from me with a hard slap, to the great amusement of Massasoit.

After much discussion, Governor Carver and Massasoit made a solemn peace treaty between our peoples. Then they embraced and exchanged gifts as if they were old friends.

When Massasoit and his men left, Squanto stayed with us. He said Patuxet was his home.

THE MAYFLOWER
RETURNS TO ENGLAND

With the worst of the winter over, Master Jones decided that he could finally sail his ship back to England. As we loaded the shallop with supplies for the ship, Bob told me that he would welcome another hand. "There's nothing for you here, lad. Come back to London with us."

But I had yet three years of my service with Governor Carver. It was not my choice to make. Bob wrapped a strong arm around my shoulder. "When you get to London, you come and find me down Southwick way, d'you hear? You'll find your fortune—don't you worry, John."

Lizzy Tilley overheard me talking to Bob about London, and she gave me a cross look.

Everyone turned out to watch the *Mayflower* as she slowly tacked around the bay and sailed over the horizon.

Squanto

We set to work planting our crops and tending our fields. Squanto showed us how to manure the ground with the little fish that we caught in great abundance. He showed us how to sow beans and squash along with the corn. One day he trod eels, fat and sweet, out of the mud with his feet and flipped them up into his hands like a magic trick. Our people were right glad when we came home that night with dozens of them.

When I joshed him about sounding like a Londoner, he told me the story of how he had been stolen to be sold as a slave by an English captain. He'd managed to escape and had spent years in London, where he'd served a good master, much as I served Governor Carver here.

"But London was not my home, and I am no man's servant. I never stopped trying to find a way to get back to Patuxet. I went on ships to America as a guide, and when I knew I was close I took my chance to get home. But when I arrived there, I found only graves and bones. All of my people had died of a plague. A white man's disease."

Squanto was silent for a while. Then he said, "Well, John Howland, if I speak like an Englishman, why is it that you, who are English, speak like a Dutchman!" and we were laughing again.

THE DEATH OF CARVER

The work in the fields was backbreaking. Squanto watched. He said it was woman's work. There were so many stones to clear away, and the weeds grew back as quickly as we could pull them up. At the end of each working day, we had to soak our aching hands in the cold water of the brook. I thought how Roger had wanted his own parcel of land here. A parcel of nettles and stones.

On a fine day, not a month after the ship had left, Master Carver himself took sick while he was out working in the fields, and within a few days, he died. He'd been our leader and our governor, and he'd been a good master to me. He even left me a sum of money in his will. His death was much lamented, and we buried him in the best manner we could with some volleys of shot from all those with muskets.

It was hard on Mistress Carver. She took sick herself then and died five weeks later.

"They are saying it was a broken heart that she died of, Master Howland," Lizzy Tilley said to me as we buried my mistress. "She loved her husband that much."

"She loved him true, Miss Tilley, but it was this wretched country that killed them both!" I answered. Lizzy looked hurt, and I was sorry I had been so sharp with her.

Now I was left without a master. I was a free and equal man.

THANKSGIVING

We chose William Bradford to be our next governor. Under his leadership, we worked hard that summer, building more houses and tending our crops. The barley and peas we brought across the sea did not thrive, but, God be praised, our Indian corn flourished.

The governor ordered me and three others to go fowling so that we might have a special celebration after we had gathered in our harvest. Squanto showed us the best places to hunt, so we came back with as many birds as we could carry. Turkeys, partridges, and quails—enough to feed us all for a week. We finally had enough to eat and more to store up for the coming winter.

Having lived through the trials of the past year, we gave thanks with a harvest festival. The feasting and merrymaking were just getting under way when Massasoit and ninety of his men entered our settlement.

I won't say we weren't a bit nervous with so many warriors around, but we welcomed them among us, and once everyone had a bit to eat and a glass of aquavit, we were all best of friends.

Massasoit's men carried in five fine deer to add to our feast. We entertained one another and feasted together for three days. I helped Lizzy carry the platters of food, and I considered myself to be most useful. "I don't know what you are smiling about, Master Howland," she scolded. "There are a half a dozen quail burning on that spit, and look — the governor's spaniel is about to steal a whole turkey."

I rushed to retrieve the turkey and burned my fingers saving the quail, which earned me a smile from Lizzy.

During a quiet moment on the third day, Elder Brewster stood and addressed us all. "Friends, let us come before the Lord with thanksgiving. Let us shout joyfully to the rock of our salvation, for He has delivered us from hunger and suffering and danger. Look now how we are blessed with fruitful fields and the choicest bounties of Heaven. Let us give thanks for our good friend and neighbor Massasoit, and for Squanto. Squanto is a special instrument sent by God for our good far beyond our expectation."

Squanto translated the bit about himself for Massasoit with the greatest pride, and he may have added a few flourishes, for he took a long time over it. In truth, without Squanto's help and wisdom, we would not have survived the year.

THE FORTUNE

With the harvest in and our celebration over, there was still plenty of work to be done. We were hoping to have two more houses built and watertight before the winter snows came.

I was working on the roof of a house for Dr. Fuller when Captain Standish shouted from the fort, "Ship ahoy!"

I nearly dropped my hammer on Dr. Fuller's head in my haste to get down the ladder. This was the first ship in our harbor since the *Mayflower* had anchored there a full year before. She was called the *Fortune*.

We had hoped for supplies from England, but all we got were thirty-five new settlers without so much as a biscuit-cake or a barrel of beer between them. They were mostly wild young men, too. Governor Bradford dispersed them between several families, and we were all put on half allowance of food to get us through the winter.

The ship's master wanted to be off again smartly, so we loaded in salted fish, sassafras timber, and two hogsheads of beaver pelts. This was a valuable cargo that would go a long way toward paying our debt to our backers.

I thought hard on things. I was a free man with money in my purse. And here was the *Fortune* that was about to return to London. London, where a hardworking young man might make something of himself, and where I might see my family and hear my mother's gentle voice again.

I resolved to take my passage home.

My friends all came to say farewell. They were sad to see me go, but they didn't try to stop me. Lizzy Tilley came, too.

"I hear you are going back to London, John Howland. Dr. Fuller's house isn't yet finished. Look—the roof is still open on both sides, and the daubing of the walls hasn't even been started yet!"

"The doctor has plenty of help. Those new boys off the ship can lend a hand," I answered. "You should come back too, Lizzy. You have no kin here. There is only another hard and hungry winter ahead of you now."

"My family is here! Buried here. Planted in American soil," said Lizzy, trying to control her temper. "They wanted to build something good here, and they died trying. They shall not have died in vain, Master Howland! You go back to England. I'm not leaving."

With that, she turned and walked away from me. I thought hard on it again. I thought about London. I thought about Master Carver and Roger, and about Squanto and Massasoit and all my friends, and what we had been through together. I thought of a rope lit up by lightning in the darkness under the icy waves. Why was I saved? To go back to London and make myself a fortune? Or to stay here and help put a roof on Dr. Fuller's house, and maybe to help build something bigger, something better? I thought again about my family. Most of all, though, I thought about Lizzy Tilley.

I turned my back on the *Fortune*. And I went up the hill to Dr. Fuller's house and I picked up my hammer.

BIBLIOGRAPHY

BOOKS

Bradford, William. *Of Plymouth Plantation, 1620–1647*. New York: Modern Library, 1981.

Charlton, Warwick. *The Voyage of the Mayflower II*. London: Cassell, 1957.

Philbrick, Nathaniel. *The Mayflower and the Pilgrims' New World*. New York: Putnam, 2008.

———. *A Story of Courage, Community, and War*. New York: Viking, 2006.

Winslow, Edward. *Mourt's Relation; or, Journal of the Plantation at Plymouth*. New York: Garrett, 1969.

FOR YOUNGER READERS

Cunningham, Kevin, and Peter Benoit. *The Wampanoag*. New York: Scholastic, 2011.

Goodman, Susan E. *Pilgrims of Plymouth*. Washington, DC: National Geographic, 2001.

Grace, Catherine O'Neill, and Margaret M. Bruchac. *1621: A New Look at Thanksgiving*. Washington, DC: National Geographic Society, 2001.

Plimoth Plantation. *Mayflower, 1620: A New Look at a Pilgrim Voyage*. Washington, DC: National Geographic Society, 2003.

Waters, Kate. *On the Mayflower*. Photographs by Russ Kendall. New York: Scholastic, 1996.

———. *Tapenum's Day: A Wampanoag Indian Boy in Pilgrim Times*. Photographs by Russ Kendall. New York: Scholastic, 1996.

WEBSITES

The Pilgrim John Howland Society: http://www.pilgrimjohnhowlandsociety.org/

Plimoth Plantation: http://www.plimoth.org/

Author's Note

It was fortunate for John Howland that he did not try to return to England on the *Fortune*. On the voyage home she, and her valuable cargo, were taken by French pirates. It was also fortunate for the Plymouth Colony, because John Howland went on to become one of its foremost citizens.

John never did return to England, and he never saw his mother again, but a few years later, his brothers, Arthur and Henry, followed him across the Atlantic Ocean to Plymouth and settled close by him.

A year or two after the events described in this book, John Howland and Elizabeth Tilley were married. They lived together for fifty years until John died in 1672 or 1673. Elizabeth lived on for fifteen more years. It seems they had a loving marriage. It was certainly a fruitful one. They had ten children and eighty-eight grandchildren. Many millions of people living in America today are descended from them.

The peace between the Wampanoag and the English settlers endured throughout John Howland's long life.

TO KAREN LOTZ

ACKNOWLEDGMENTS

With thanks to my many models, particularly Diarmaid, Cia, William, and Rubén.

Thanks also to Dylan, Ben, Sam, Evie, Barbara, Johnny, Joe, and Jacq, and to
Ann Kavanagh of the Young People's Theatre, Dublin.

I greatly appreciate the patient guidance of Hilary, Chris, and Lisa at Candlewick Press,
as well as the continuing care of my agent, Clare Conville.

Lastly I want to acknowledge the invaluable support of the Literature Bursary
awarded to me by the Arts Council of Ireland to assist me in the completion of this book.

First edition 2015

Library of Congress Catalog Card Number 2014952482
ISBN 978-0-7636-6584-5

15 16 17 18 19 20 APS 10 9 8 7 6 5 4 3 2 1
Printed in Humen, Dongguan, China

This book was typeset in Columbus MT.
The illustrations were done in watercolor and gouache.

Candlewick Press
99 Dover Street
Somerville, Massachusetts 02144

visit us at www.candlewick.com